Date: 10/1/20

J BIO CURIE
Raum, Elizabeth,
The life of Marie Curie /

THE LIFE OF

MARIE CURIE

BY ELIZABETH RAUM

AMICUS | AMICUS INK

Sequence is published by Amicus and Amicus Ink
P.O. Box 1329, Mankato, MN 56002
www.amicuspublishing.us

Library of Congress Cataloging-in-Publication Data
Names: Raum, Elizabeth, author.
Title: The Life of Marie Curie / by Elizabeth Raum.
Description: Mankato, Minnesota : Amicus, [2020] | Series: Sequence. Change maker biographies | Audience: K to grade 3. | Includes bibliographical references and index.
Identifiers: LCCN 2018028198 (print) | LCCN 2018035304 (ebook) | ISBN 9781681517605 (pdf) | ISBN 9781681516783 (library binding) | ISBN 9781681524641 (pbk.)
Subjects: LCSH: Curie, Marie, 1867-1934--Juvenile literature. | Women chemists--Poland--Biography--Juvenile literature. | Women chemists--France--Biography--Juvenile literature. | Scientists--France--Biography--Juvenile literature. | Radioactivity--Juvenile literature. | Nobel Prize winners--Biography--Juvenile literature.
Classification: LCC QD22.C8 (ebook) | LCC QD22.C8 R3825 2020 (print) | DDC 540.92 [B] --dc23
LC record available at https://lccn.loc.gov/2018028198

Editor: Alissa Thielges
Designer: Ciara Beitlich
Photo Researcher: Holly Young

Photo Credits: Age Fotostock/Ann Ronan Pictures cover; SuperStock/alb318362 cover; Getty/Science Source 4; WikiCommons/Unknown Photographer 7; Mary Evans/Mary Evans Picture Library 8–9, 16; Shutterstock/Everett Historical 10; Flickr/Energy Fuels Inc./Nuclear Regulatory Commission 13; Getty/abadonian 13; Shutterstock/Imagewell 13; Shutterstock/concept w 14; Shutterstock/TonelloPhotography 14; WikiCommons/Weirdmeister 14; WikiCommons/LOC Flickr 19; Getty/The Print Collector 20–21; WikiCommons 20–21; Mary Evans/The Royal College of Nursing Archive Collection 22–23; Alamy/GL Archive 25; Alamy/For Alan 26; Getty/John Phillips/The LIFE Picture Collection 28–29; Shutterstock/Huang, Zheng 29

Printed in the United States of America

HC 10 9 8 7 6 5 4 3 2 1
PB 10 9 8 7 6 5 4 3 2 1

TABLE OF CONTENTS

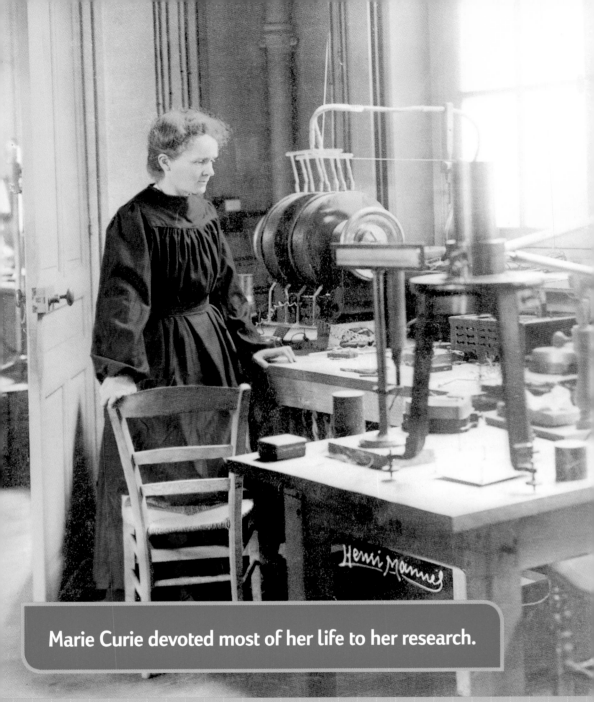

Marie Curie devoted most of her life to her research.

Who was Marie Curie?

Marie Curie was a scientist. She studied **radiation**. She found that certain **atoms** caused this kind of energy. Her work led to many important discoveries about atomic energy. Marie won two **Nobel Prizes**. One was in **physics**. The other was in chemistry. Marie's work led to new cures for cancer.

Finding a Way to Learn

Marie Curie was born in Warsaw, Poland, on November 7, 1867. Her birth name was Maria Sklodowska. Her parents were teachers. Maria was first in her high school class. But girls in Poland could not go to college. Instead, Maria got a job. She studied on her own.

Marie Curie is born.

NOV. 7, 1867

Marie, age 16 here, dreamed of getting a college degree.

LOADING...LOADING...LOADING...

In 1891, Maria moved to Paris. She called herself Marie, the French name for Maria. She studied at the **Sorbonne**. This is a famous college in Paris. In only two years, she earned degrees in math and physics. After college, she went back to Poland. She wanted to teach college. But no one would hire a woman.

The Sorbonne was known for its art and science programs.

Marie Curie is born.

NOV. 7, 1867   1891

DING...LOADING...

Marie moves to Paris.

Marie Curie is born.

Marie marries Pierre Curie.

NOV. 7, 1867   1891   1895

...LOADING...

Marie moves to Paris.

Working with Pierre

Marie returned to Paris to do research. She shared a lab with another scientist, Pierre Curie. They worked together. In June 1895, they married. Pierre taught at the Sorbonne. Marie wanted to teach in Paris. But women weren't allowed to teach there.

Pierre and Marie continued to work together after marrying.

Marie began studying a metal called **uranium**. It gave off strange rays. The atoms in the metal gave off an electric charge. Marie **coined** a new word: **radioactive**. She combined the words active and radiation.

Uranium is a metal. It is used as fuel to make nuclear energy.

Marie Curie is born.

Marie marries Pierre Curie.

NOV. 7, 1867   1891   1895   1898

OADING . . .

Marie moves to Paris.

Marie coins the word "radioactive."

88
(226)
Ra
RADIUM

89-
Ac-
Actir

127.6

84

18
32
18
6

Po

Polonium

[209]

Astatine

[210]

18
32
18
7

Marie Curie is born.	Marie marries Pierre Curie.	Curies report on new elements, polonium and radium.

NOV. 7, 1867   1891   1895   1898   DEC. 1898

Marie moves to Paris.	Marie coins the word "radioactive."

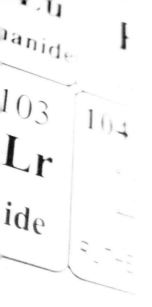

The Curies found that **pitchblende** was more radioactive than uranium. It contained two new **elements**. They called one polonium, named after Poland. They called the other radium. They found that radium destroyed cancer cells faster than healthy cells. They reported their findings in December 1898.

Pitchblende is black and solid at room temperature.

LOADING...LOADING...LOADING...

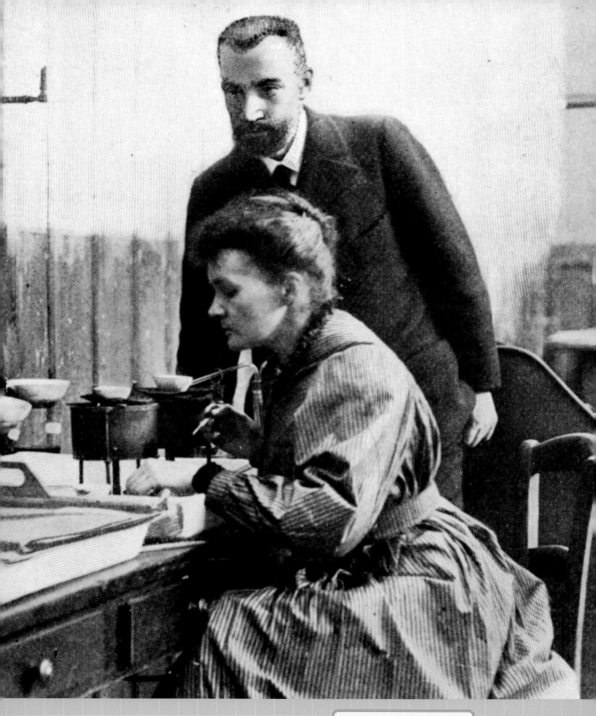

Marie Curie is born.

Marie marries Pierre Curie.

Curies report on new elements, polonium and radium.

NOV. 7, 1867   1891   1895   1898   DEC. 1898   1903

Marie moves to Paris.

Marie coins the word "radioactive."

Marie is the first woman to win a Nobel Prize.

In 1903, the Curies won a Nobel Prize in physics. The prize was for their research in radiation. Marie was the first woman to win a Nobel Prize. Other winners gave speeches. Not Marie. Women were not allowed to speak.

The Curies' lab was an old shed. They lived and worked in Paris.

Marie on Her Own

In 1906, Pierre was killed in a wagon accident. Marie was shocked and sad. Even so, she kept working. Her work honored Pierre. Marie became the head of the lab. She took over his teaching job, too. Marie was the first woman to teach at the Sorbonne.

Marie Curie is born.

Marie marries Pierre Curie.

Curies report on new elements, polonium and radium.

NOV. 7, 1867   1891   1895   1898   DEC. 1898   1903

Marie moves to Paris.

Marie coins the word "radioactive."

Marie is the first woman to win a Nobel Prize.

Marie (center) sits with some of the students she taught.

Marie becomes the first female teacher at the Sorbonne.

1906

LOADING... LOADING...

Marie Curie is born.

Marie marries Pierre Curie.

Curies report on new elements, polonium and radium.

NOV. 7, 1867　　1891　　1895　　1898　　DEC. 1898　　1903

Marie moves to Paris.

Marie coins the word "radioactive."

Marie is the first woman to win a Nobel Prize.

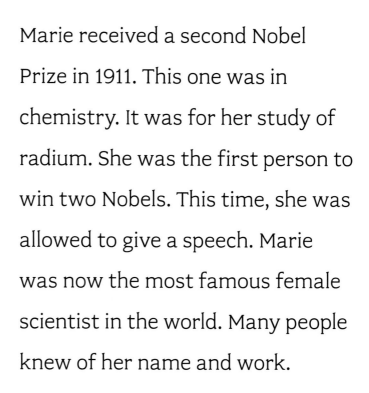

Marie received a second Nobel Prize in 1911. This one was in chemistry. It was for her study of radium. She was the first person to win two Nobels. This time, she was allowed to give a speech. Marie was now the most famous female scientist in the world. Many people knew of her name and work.

This is Marie's Nobel Prize award. Her research was used to help treat cancer.

Marie becomes the first female teacher at the Sorbonne.

1906   1911

...DING... LOADING...

Marie wins Nobel Prize in chemistry; first person to win two Nobels.

Marie Curie is born.

Marie marries Pierre Curie.

Curies report on new elements, polonium and radium.

NOV. 7, 1867   1891   1895   1898   DEC. 1898   1903

Marie moves to Paris.

Marie coins the word "radioactive."

Marie is the first woman to win a Nobel Prize.

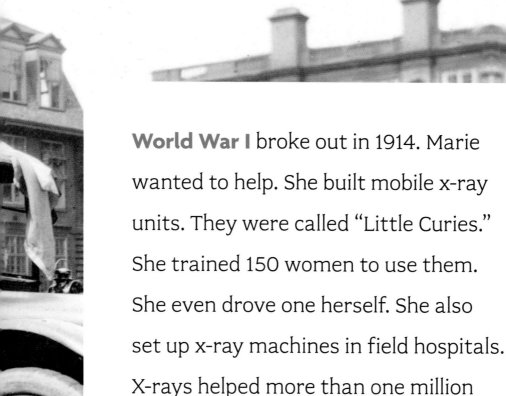

World War I broke out in 1914. Marie wanted to help. She built mobile x-ray units. They were called "Little Curies." She trained 150 women to use them. She even drove one herself. She also set up x-ray machines in field hospitals. X-rays helped more than one million wounded soldiers.

Each Little Curie was made with donated cars and equipment.

Marie becomes the first female teacher at the Sorbonne.

Marie sets up mobile x-ray units.

1906   1911   1914–1918

. . . LOADING . . .

Marie wins Nobel Prize in chemistry; first person to win two Nobels.

Worldwide Fame

The war ended in 1918. Marie went back to her lab at the Radium Institute. But radium was costly. She traveled the world to raise money. She spoke in Belgium, Brazil, and Spain. In the United States, Marie met President Warren G. Harding. He gave her a small amount of radium to use in her lab.

Marie Curie is born.

Marie marries Pierre Curie.

Curies report on new elements, polonium and radium.

| NOV. 7, 1867 | 1891 | 1895 | 1898 | DEC. 1898 | 1903 |

Marie moves to Paris.

Marie coins the word "radioactive."

Marie is the first woman to win a Nobel Prize.

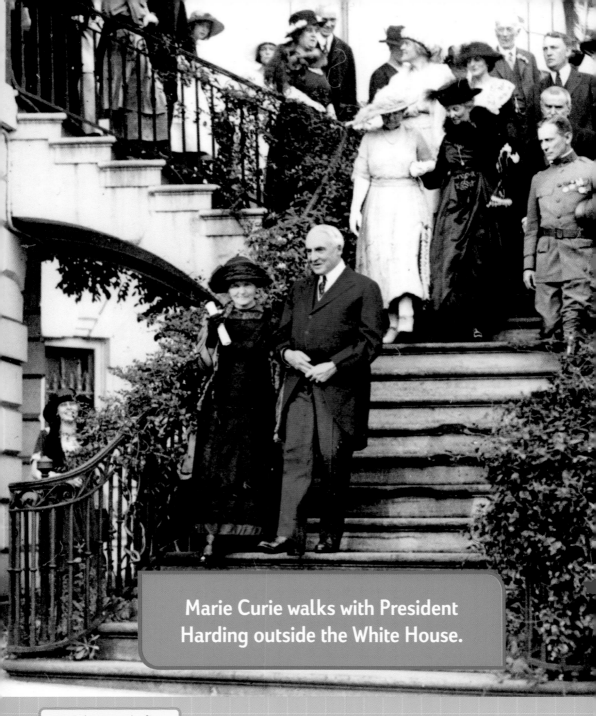

Marie Curie walks with President Harding outside the White House.

Marie becomes the first female teacher at the Sorbonne.

Marie sets up mobile x-ray units.

1906   1911   1914-1918   1918-1921

Marie wins Nobel Prize in chemistry; first person to win two Nobels.

Marie raises money for research.

Marie Curie is born.

Marie marries Pierre Curie.

Curies report on new elements, polonium and radium.

NOV. 7, 1867   1891   1895   1898   DEC. 1898   1903

Marie moves to Paris.

Marie coins the word "radioactive."

Marie is the first woman to win a Nobel Prize.

In 1922, Marie joined the French Academy of Medicine. This group works to improve medical care. Marie was the first female member. She kept working in her lab. But she was often ill. Marie had a blood disease often caused by too much radiation. She died on July 4, 1934. She was 66 years old.

Marie's illness was due to radiation. She worked with it while unprotected.

Marie becomes the first female teacher at the Sorbonne.

Marie sets up mobile x-ray units.

Marie dies of blood disease.

| 1906 | 1911 | 1914-1918 | 1918-1921 | JULY 4, 1934 |

Marie wins Nobel Prize in chemistry; first person to win two Nobels.

Marie raises money for research.

Today, Marie Curie's name is known all over the world. The Radium Institute is now the Curie Institute. Others continue Marie's work. They have discovered new uses for radiation. In 1944, Glen Seaborg discovered a new element. It was radioactive. He named it curium in honor of the Curies.

The Radium Institute in Paris bears Marie Curie's name. In Warsaw, Poland, a statue honors her discovery of polonium.

Marie Curie is born.

Marie marries Pierre Curie.

Curies report on new elements, polonium and radium.

NOV. 7, 1867   1891   1895   1898   DEC. 1898   1903

Marie moves to Paris.

Marie coins the word "radioactive."

Marie is the first woman to win a Nobel Prize.

Marie becomes the first female teacher at the Sorbonne.

Marie sets up mobile x-ray units.

Marie dies of blood disease.

1906 1911 1914–1918 1918–1921 JULY 4, 1934 1944

Marie wins Nobel Prize in chemistry; first person to win two Nobels.

Marie raises money for research.

Curium named in honor of the Curies.

29

Glossary

atom The smallest part of an element that still contains all the properties of the element.

coin To create a new word.

element A substance, like gold, that cannot be broken down into simpler substances.

Nobel Prize A prize awarded each year to people who make important discoveries in the fields of literature, physics, chemistry, medicine, economics, and world peace.

physics A science that deals with matter and energy.

pitchblende A black mineral that contains uranium and radium.

radiation The energy produced by radioactive elements like uranium.

radioactive When a material is giving off harmful radiation from atoms that have broken down.

Sorbonne A university in Paris.

uranium A silver-white radioactive metal used in nuclear energy.

World War I A war fought from 1914 to 1918 mainly in Europe. The United States, Great Britain, France, Russia, Italy, Japan and other allied nations defeated Germany, Austria-Hungary, Turkey, and Bulgaria.

Read More

Demi. *Marie Curie.* New York: Henry Holt and Company, 2018.

Krieg, Katherine. *Marie Curie: Physics and Chemistry Pioneer.* Minneapolis: Core Library, 2015.

O'Quinn, Amy M. *Marie Curie for Kids: Her Life and Scientific Discoveries, with 21 Activities and Experiments.* Chicago: Chicago Review Press, 2017.

Websites

Ducksters | Biography: Marie Curie
https://www.ducksters.com/biography/women_leaders/marie_curie.php

Marie Curie: Her Story in Brief
https://history.aip.org/exhibits/curie/brief/index.html

The Nobel Prize | Marie Curie: Facts
https://www.nobelprize.org/prizes/physics/1903/marie-curie/facts/

Index

About the Author

Elizabeth Raum has written over 100 books for young readers. Many are biographies. She enjoys learning about people who help us see the world in new and exciting ways. She lives in Fargo, North Dakota. To learn more, visit her website: www.ElizabethRaumBooks.com.